RUBANK EDUCATIONAL LIBRARY No. 57

RUBANK Elementary METHOD

MARIMBA or XYLOPHONE

HOWARD M. PETERSON

A FUNDAMENTAL COURSE FOR INDIVIDUAL OR LIKE-INSTRUMENT CLASS INSTRUCTION

RUBANK®

HAL•LEONARD®
CORPORATION
7777 W. BLUEMOUND RD. P.O. BOX 13819 MILWAUKEE, WI 53213

Preliminary Explanations

The Keyboard and Notes on the Staff

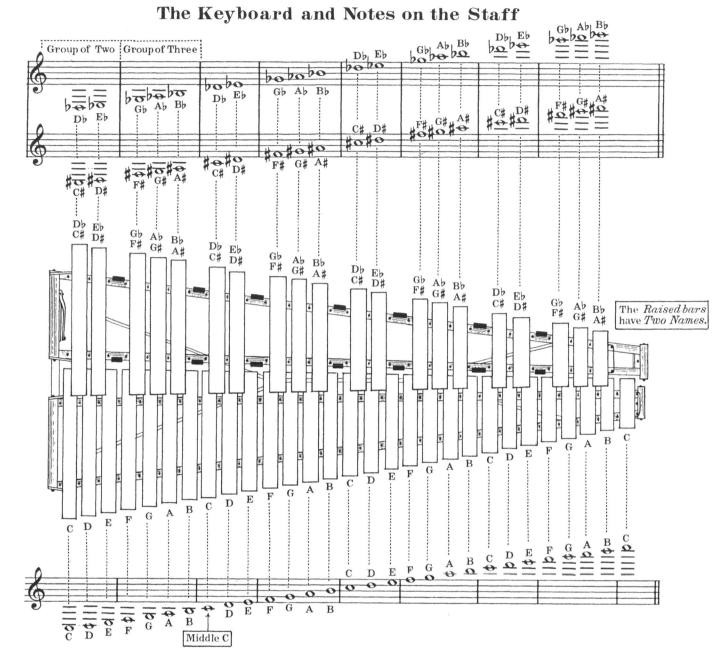

Fig. 1

The keyboard of a four-octave instrument, C to C.

All bars on the instrument and notes on the staff are named by a letter of the MUSIC ALPHABET: A, B, C, D, E, F, G, (with necessary sharps or flats). Fig. 1 shows the relation of the keyboard to the notes on the staff.

Table of notes and rests

Musical sounds are represented by characters called NOTES. The lines and spaces of the staff indicate the *pitch* and *name* of the tones represented by the notes written upon them. The form of a note determines its *time-value*. RESTS indicate silence of measured duration. For each note there is a corresponding Rest.

ONE Whole Note,	𝅝 =			
equals *two* Half Notes,	𝅗𝅥	𝅗𝅥 =		
or *four* Quarter Notes,	♩	♩ ♩ ♩ =		
or *eight* Eighth Notes,	♪ ♪ ♪ ♪	𝅘𝅥𝅮𝅘𝅥𝅮𝅘𝅥𝅮𝅘𝅥𝅮 =		
or *sixteen* Sixteenth Notes,	𝅘𝅥𝅯 𝅘𝅥𝅯 𝅘𝅥𝅯 𝅘𝅥𝅯	𝅘𝅥𝅯𝅘𝅥𝅯𝅘𝅥𝅯𝅘𝅥𝅯𝅘𝅥𝅯𝅘𝅥𝅯𝅘𝅥𝅯𝅘𝅥𝅯 =		

ONE Whole Rest,	▬ =			
equals *two* Half Rests,	▬	▬ =		
or *four* Quarter Rests,	𝄽	𝄽 𝄽	𝄽 =	
or *eight* Eighth Rests,	𝄾 𝄾 𝄾	𝄾 𝄾 𝄾 𝄾 𝄾 =		
or *sixteen* Sixteenth Rests,	𝄿𝄿𝄿𝄿𝄿𝄿𝄿𝄿 𝄿𝄿𝄿𝄿𝄿𝄿𝄿𝄿			

Copyright MCMXXXVIII by Rubank Inc., Chicago, Ill.
International Copyright Secured

Copyright Renewed

How to Hold the Hammers

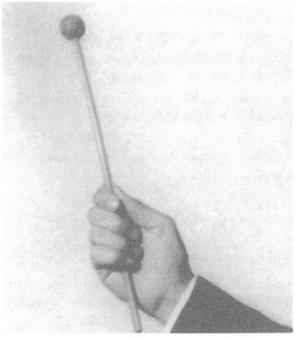

Fig. 2

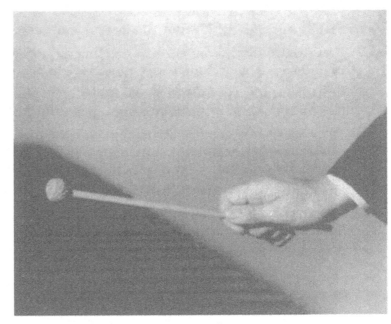

Fig. 3

The hammer is held between the THUMB and the FIRST JOINT OF THE INDEX FINGER. The power of the HOLD must come at this point. The remaining fingers are closed over the hammer, the tips almost touching the palm, but NOT TOO TIGHTLY; they give only GENTLE SUPPORT to keep the hammer in position.

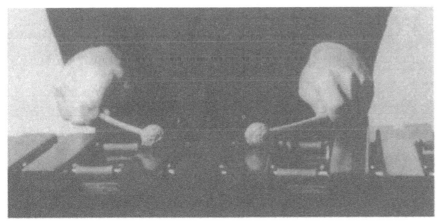

Fig. 4

In playing position (*Fig. 4*), the hands are held quite level, fingers turned well under, thumb held firmly against the hammer, and the hands are LOW. The WRIST is used in making a stroke. Do not raise the hammers too high.

The Roll

The ROLL consists of a series of ALTERNATING SINGLE STROKES of the hammers to sustain a tone, the strokes alternated as *rapidly* and *evenly* as possible. Use the wrists to raise the hammers, do not raise one hammer any higher than the other, and move the hammers straight up and down. The Roll is indicated by lines drawn over or under a note, or across the stem, as: ≅, ♩, ♪.

Daily Practice

Practice the Roll on all bars, in chromatic order, beginning with *Middle C bar* up to the *high C bar* two octaves above. Do not count the strokes, start slowly, gradually faster, then as fast as possible with an *even power of stroke.* STOP and relax before starting on the next higher bar.

BAR: C   C   C   C   C   C C C CCCCCCCCC, etc. *Faster and faster.*
HAND: *L*   *R*   *L*   *R*   *L*   *R   L R   LRLRLRLRLR*, etc. STOP — relax.

C♯ C♯ C♯ C♯ C♯ C♯ C♯ C♯C♯C♯C♯C♯C♯C♯C♯C♯C♯,etc. *Faster and faster.*
L   R   L   R   L   R   L R L R L R L R L R L R,etc. STOP — relax.

(Continue up the keyboard in chromatic order to *high C bar*, then come DOWN on each bar to *Middle C bar*.)

4

Points to Remember

1. Keep the hands and hammers LOW.

2. Stand near the CENTER of the instrument, a few inches away from the edge of the bars.

3. Practice the Roll from *slow to fast,* in every practice period, until it has been developed to an automatic process. A good Roll is very important in playing the Xylophone and Marimba.

4. Roll on bars to the *left* of the body center by placing the RIGHT HAMMER in *front* of the left; on bars to the *right* of the body center, place the LEFT HAMMER in front of the right.

5. The *raised bars* may be struck on the END or in the center. Practice the Roll TWO WAYS on the raised bars; 1st, both hammers in the *center;* 2nd, one hammer placed in the *center* and the other hammer on the *end.* In the lower row, always strike the bars in the center.

6. Constantly review the PROPER POSITIONS.

7. Use the WRISTS. There must be a minimum of arm movement up and down. Lift the hammer QUICK-LY off the bar once the tone has been sounded.

8. Give each note its proper time-value. Count correctly and retain a steady tempo.

Treble Staff

Quarter Notes – Quarter Rests

In 4/4 or "Common Time," there are *four counts* to each measure. Each Quarter Note or Quarter Rest receives one count.

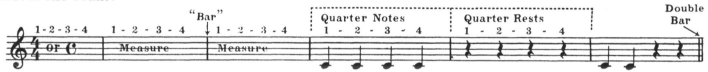

In Exercises No. 1, 2 and 3, first play all notes with the *left hand only;* second, all notes with the *right hand only;* third, *play as marked* (L or R). Practice each way several times.

COUNT: 1 - 2 - 3 - 4   1-2-3-4   1-2-3-4   1-2-3-4   1-2-3-4   1-2-3-4   1-2-3-4   1-2-3-4

(Observe the hammering as marked)

Quarter Notes – Quarter Rests (Continued)

Whole Notes – Whole Rests

Sustain each Whole Note with an even ROLL to its full value of *four counts*. Count "1-2-3-4" to each measure. Play slowly and evenly.

★ At this point, it is recommended that "Music for Marimba, Vol. I," by Art Jolliff, be introduced as supplementary melodic material.

High Notes

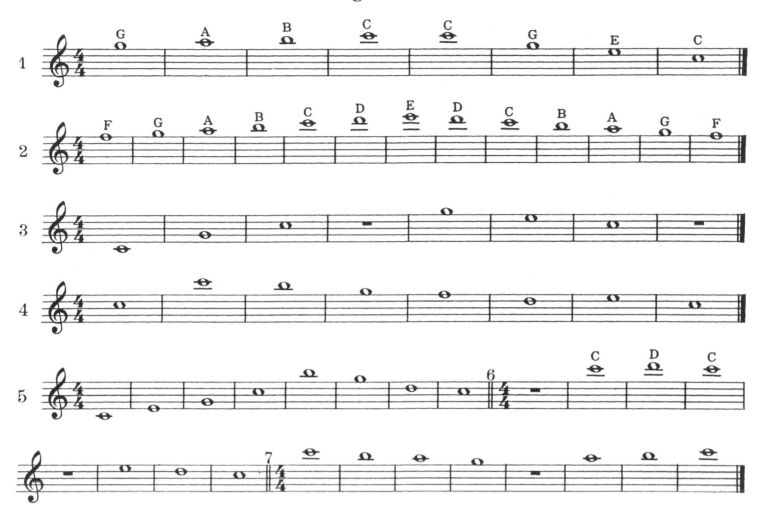

Half Notes – Half Rests

Repeat each exercise several times. Roll all notes. Each Half Note or Half Rest receives two counts.

8

Whole and Half Notes

Wide Jumps

Melody

Whole, Half and Quarter Notes

Melody

Counting Exercise

10

Dotted Half Notes

A dotted Half Note receives *three counts*: 𝅗𝅥 𝅗𝅥 = 𝅗𝅥.

Roll the dotted Half Notes.

Melody

Melody

Melody

Melody

Eighth Notes – Eighth Rests

Two Eighth Notes or Eighth Rests equal one Quarter Note:

Play the following exercises (No. 3 to 9) first with *L.H. alone*; second, *R.H. alone*; then *Hand to Hand* as marked (L or R). Count aloud.

271-48

Observe the hammering.

The Slur

The Slur affects notes on *different* lines or spaces; the Tie, notes on the same line or space.

Connect the notes.

(Roll all notes)

Roll all notes.

Roll all notes.

Staccato and Legato

Phrase mark

Technical Development and Reading

First, play all notes with the *Left Hand alone*; second, *Right Hand alone*; third, *roll all notes* ★

★ NOTE: This plan of practice has these purposes: 1st, to develop the ROLL to a high degree; 2nd, to develop a LEGATO STYLE of playing; 3rd, to develop either hand, and 4th, for the development of SIGHT READING.

Technical Development and Reading (continued)

First, play all notes with the *L.H. alone*; second, *R.H. alone*; third, *Roll all Quarter Notes* and strike the *Eighth Notes* with the hammer as indicated (L or R).

Introducing Double Notes

Middle Register

Low Register

Technical Development and Reading (continued)

Middle Register

Low Register

Three-Four Time ("Waltz Time")

Melody

Exercises in Three-Four Time

NOTE: First, *L.H. alone*; second, *R.H. alone*; third, *roll* all notes except eighth notes which are struck with the designated hammer (L-R).

18

Good Night Ladies

Waltz

Waltz

Waltz

Dotted Quarter Notes

Come, All Ye Faithful
(Adeste Fideles)

Traditional

Key of G Major

Two-Four Time

America

Introducing Accidentals

Key of F Major

Blue Bells of Scotland

Scotch Folk Song

Study in Double Notes

Observe the Accidentals.
Roll all notes

Waltz

Roll all notes

Key of B♭ Major

Memorize.
B♭ MAJOR SCALE

B♭ MAJOR CHORD

271-48

22

Melody in B♭

Old Hundred

How Can I Leave Thee

Silent Night, Holy Night

Key of E♭ Major

Auld Lang Syne

Scotch Folk Song

Key of D Major

Key of A Major

26

Alla Breve ("Cut Time")

271-48

Six - Eight Time

First, count *six* to a measure. Accent counts *1* and *4*. Second, count *two* to a measure; the first beat falls on count "1", the second beat on count "4", like this: *1-2-3-4-5-6*

271-48

28

Exercises in Tied Notes

Sixteenth Notes

Roll the Half Notes

271-48

Study

Melody

Dotted Eighth Notes

Exercises in Sixteenth Notes

Exercises in 6/8 Time

Sweet and Low

J. Barnby

Believe Me, If All Those Endearing Young Charms

Moore

Love's Old Sweet Song

Duke Street

Chromatic Scale

STRIKE THE RAISED BARS ON THE ENDS

Play *smoothly* and *evenly*.
Play *Hand to Hand* throughout (L,R,L,R, etc. or R,L,R,L, etc.)

Syncopation

Melody

Triplets

Dotted Eighth Notes and Triplets

Melody

Melody

Rests – Tied Notes

Tone – Expression

Double Notes

Thirds

The double notes not rolled must be struck *exactly together*.

Varied Intervals

Sixths

Double Notes (continued)

Wrist and Stroke Development

Play fast and evenly.

Strike double notes exactly together.

Minuet – "Don Juan"

Moderato

W. A. Mozart

My Maryland

Gavotte

Gossec

Come Back to Erin

C. Barnard

40

Broken Thirds

Study

Roll Exercises – Wide Jumps

Roll all notes. Do not strike any bars in between each jump.

Favor a *short roll* on each Quarter Note.

Practice Routine :
1. L.H. alone.
2. R.H. alone.
3. Both hands as marked (L or R).

Line Etudes

(Optional hammering.)

Space Etudes

Holy, Holy, Holy

John B. Dykes

Onward, Christian Soldiers

A. S. Sullivan

Lead, Kindly Light

John B. Dykes

Rock of Ages

Thos. Hastings

There is a Green Hill Far Away

Geo. C. Stebbins

In the Gloaming – Duet

Roll all notes.

Annie Laurie – Duet

Roll all notes.

All Through the Night – Duet

(Roll all notes.)

Old Song – Ensemble

(Roll all notes.)

NOTE: These arrangements for Ensemble may be used for two, three or four part playing.

Old Black Joe – Ensemble

Swanee River – Ensemble

(Roll all notes.)

Drink to Me Only With Thine Eyes – Ensemble

(Roll all notes.)

Major Scales – Chords

Memorize all scales and chords.

Sharp Keys